DANGER DAYS

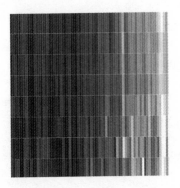

CATHERINE PIERCE

Distributed by Independent Publishers Group
Chicago

Saturnalia Books
105 Woodside Rd.
Ardmore, PA 19003
info@saturnaliabooks.com

ISBN: 978-1-947817-20-3 (print), 978-1-947817-21-0 (ebook)
Library of Congress Control Number: 2020941793
Book design: Robin Vuchnich
Cover Illustration: David Curran
Printing by Versa Press

Distributed by:
Independent Publishing Group
814 N. Franklin St.
Chicago, IL 60610
800-888-4741

CONTENTS

ooooo

ooooo

for my mother
and my father

someone will remember us
        I say
          even in another time

—Sappho, trans. Anne Carson

ANTHROPOCENE PASTORAL

In the beginning, the ending was beautiful.
Early spring everywhere, the trees furred
pink and white, lawns the sharp green
that meant *new*. The sky so blue it looked
manufactured. Robins. We'd heard
the cherry blossoms wouldn't blossom
this year, but what was one epic blooming
when even the desert was an explosion
of verbena? When bobcats slinked through
primroses. When coyotes slept deep in orange
poppies. One New Year's Day we woke
to daffodils, wisteria, onion grass wafting
through the open windows. Near the end,
we were eyeletted. We were cottoned.
We were sundressed and barefoot. *At least
it's starting gentle*, we said. An absurd comfort,
we knew, a placebo. But we were built like that.
Built to say *at least*. Built to reach for the heat
of skin on skin even when we were already hot,
built to love the purpling desert in the twilight,
built to marvel over the pink bursting dogwoods,
to hold tight to every pleasure even as we
rocked together toward the graying, even as
we held each other, warmth to warmth,
and said *sorry, I'm sorry, I'm so sorry* while petals
sifted softly to the ground all around us.

In Which the Country Is an Abandoned Amusement Park

Here is the wrecked Zipper, its cages
warrened now with rabbits and crabgrass.

Here is the splintering concession stand.
Once you bought cotton candy and gave

not a thought to how something so very
there was instantly so very *not*, only the pinging

afterfeel of sugar against your molars.
Here is the wooden coaster. Once it hurtled

down the tracks and you threw your hands
high and shrieked. It was a lark then

to be helpless, to know your car
might careen off the curve and launch

into the far-below pines, but probably not.
Here is a funhouse. How was it fun,

once, to see your face as not your face?
You try to remember, but your mouth

is so warped, and your eyes look wider
with every step. Like you could fall into them.

Like they can't believe what they're seeing.

Prayer

Dear Lord, for years I have prayed
the way a rabbit runs from a dog.
Dear Lord, I am tired. I would like to pray
by looking hard, say, at the wavering stripe
of sun on the gray ocean. I would
like to pray by carrying a wolf spider
to the yard in a juice glass. Lord, I don't know
about this feudal nomenclature. Whose
invention is that? I would like to pray
to you as River. Or Adirondacks. Or
That Moment My Son Called A Cicada Shell
My Little Guy. Or Mysterious Deep
and Moving. I hope you don't think
that's sacrilege—believe me when I say
I think I'll hear you better if I capitalize
more. Please forgive me. I am afraid
and my fear has crept like kudzu.
There is a pun to make here about
this futile nomenclature, but I don't want
to make it. So far this poem is true.
Lord, I try to be true. Lord, I love
pine needles. I love a jukebox. I love
the night my husband and I went to
a nearly-empty strip club on Bourbon Street.
Dear Lord, I don't imagine you can
be shocked. It was an October night,

and I wore a gray skirt, and we walked
back to our hotel happy, holding hands,
and that must also be prayer, all of it,
I think. Is that all right? Lord, if I call you
Fireworks Over the Lake, if I call you
These Arms of Mine on the Radio,
if I call you Soft and Untroubled
Breathing in a Bedroom with Nightlight,
will you hear me? Lord, I pray for that, too.
Not so much like the rabbit. More like
the dog, who, done with chasing,
would like to rest its head on its paws
and hear the word *Good*.

HIGH DANGEROUS

is what my sons call the flowers—
purple, white, electric blue—

pom-pomming bushes all along
the beach town streets.

I can't correct them into
hydrangeas, or I won't.

Bees ricochet in and out
of the clustered petals,

and my sons panic and dash
and I tell them about good

insects, pollination, but the truth is
I want their fear-box full of bees.

This morning the radio
said *tender age shelters*.

This morning the glaciers
are retreating. How long now

until the space-print backpack
becomes district-policy clear?

We're almost to the beach,
and *High dangerous!* my sons

yell again, their joy in having
spotted something beautiful,

and called it what it is.

In Praise of the Horror Movie

Because of the boys with their bowl cuts.
Because of the dogs yelping into the dark woods

and the horses rolling their eyes white.
Because of the mothers smoking their nerves

down to the filter. Because of the trees
with their toothed loomings. Because inside

the red-boothed diner, or the high school gym
echoing with slam dunks, or the haze

of the howling dreamscape, terror
can always be lit blue and scored.

Because when someone dies, maybe a lamp
in a log cabin goes black, or maybe

there's blood and dark-stained rags, or maybe
there's a bruised and blue body that turns out

not to be a body, or maybe someone simply
sparks into electricity and is gone, but no one

is ever making careful financial arrangements,
no one is laboring over a will unless

a long-lost son is on the scene to scavenge.
The word *escapism* is a misnomer.

It's not a getting away. It's a vanishing into.
That's you, face hidden in the corner booth.

That's you, the flickering desk lamp
at the county morgue. All around you,

someone else's world unfolds. Everyone here
is in terrible danger. That is, everyone else.

The Guilt Depot

The filing cabinets are clearly labeled:
Wrecked Vacations, Sex Lies, Domestic Road Kill.
One shelf sags under unlocked guns. Another
under melted slugs. Bookcases are lined
with the Annals of Ambivalent Motherhood.
The radio loops prom songs.
The light bulbs are all incandescent.
An industrial freezer houses the nitrated
hotdogs, deep-fried Oreos, Red Dye 40 cereals.
On the wall, a massive glistening mosaic
crafted from thrown plates. Shoeboxes full
of tiny reminder cards for missed mammograms
and colonoscopies. Shoeboxes of unsent letters,
all ending with *So now you know*. Each day
new bins are carted in. It's a plum gig for workers—
job security, hazard pay. Applicants must answer
one question: *Did you first feel remorse over*
a) stealing, b) thinking, c) a let-go balloon gone forever?
The correct answer, of course, is c: you're hireable
if each night before sleep you see that pinpoint
rising, your useless hand reaching, the blue sky
around you faultless, maddeningly clear.

PILLOW TALK

Tell me, beloved, about the eight spiders
I have swallowed in my sleep.
Make them daddy longlegs. Make them
black widows. Make one a brown recluse
snugged against my tongue then
gulped to the dark. Wrap your hands
softly in my hair and murmur
the spinnarets, the eyes upon eyes.
Last week someone scrawled swastikas
across a Fairfax JCC. Today I wrote
postcards until my hands cramped,
dear valued voter, dear neighbor. Tell me,
beloved, about hookworms, about how
walking barefoot on soft brown soil
invites the larvae in, how even now
they might be gliding down
my bloodstream, my lungs, the maze
of my small intestine. Hold me close.
This morning explosives were mailed
to the homes of famous Americans
and I'm ashamed to say that I read
the news and then forgot all about it until
a moment ago. Beloved, remember how
we used to gasp and flinch? We were sweet
then, weren't we. Tell me about the man

from Cape Cod whose lung sprouted
a pea plant—the raw pea down
the wrong pipe, the splitting, the seeding
into lobe. Pull me to you in the dark.
Murmur these charming horrors. Beloved,
let me close my eyes tonight, your hand
on my cheek light as a wolf spider.

INHERITANCE

Dear children, when we were children
the sun pushed against us and we let it.
We were not cautious. It didn't push hard.
It was only the sun, and it was ours, after all.

Dear children, when we were children
mosquitos carried nothing but annoyance.
Our Coke cans always lipped with bees.
Dear children, in winter we measured

snow drifts with yard sticks. Sometimes
ice glassed every leaf on the rhododendron.
Some of us learned to drive stick on slick
gray streets. There was that one summer

of the heatwave—we remember it because
it shifted everything a bit, the pavement
blurring, our fathers swearing over the grill.
We remember it, is what I'm saying,

like you remember anything unusual.
Dear children, when we were children
the TV sometimes droned on about ozone
and acid rain and we understood that the future

was a country our parents would have
to navigate but had nothing to do with us.
We had so many flowers. We had so many
polar bears. Our ice shelves were beautifully

intact. There were still storms, sometimes
terrible, and people died in terrible ways,
and we remember how every magazine
in the checkout line for a week that one year,

and also that other year, was stamped
with a hurricane's name, font bold and tragic.
We remember, is what I'm saying. And then
it was pure summer again, the bee-hum loud

in the fields. September like an apple split
open to its crisp, bright heart. We loved it all
as children do—roughly and distractedly—
and we continued to love it that way

as the fields slowly hushed, as snow drifts
hissed and blinked and became banks
of memory, gleaming rises of words
that we could leave to you.

How Becoming a Mother Is Like Space Travel

The astronaut told us
he didn't look out the window
for eight and a half minutes
as the rocket launched him
beyond our atmosphere.
Terrifying things happened—
ground vanished, boosters
exploded, day became
night—and he did not look.
He was focusing,
he said, on his job.

He was up there
a long time. He learned
to sleep suspended. He learned
how the sunrise looks
when you watch it every morning
from the soft dark mouth
of space. Many things,
he told us, were different
than he'd once expected.
There's no space ice cream,
he said. *That's a big hoax.*
His vision blurred.
His body became a study:
blood, appetite, cognitive function.

He took many pictures.
All of them were beautiful.
None of them showed
what it was like to float.

When the astronaut returned
to earth, more tests were run.
Scientists discovered that
seven percent of his genes
had changed in space.
He left the planet
as himself. He came back
as himself, rearranged.

STRATEGIES FOR MOTHERS IN THE AGE OF THIS AGE

For one, skip past "Sloop John B"—that flute
might send anyone right into the abyss.

Stop ferrying errant house spiders to the yard—
we can't waste our ache-space on arachnids.

If there's a solar eclipse, stay in. It's too much
to watch the erosion of light we thought was certain.

But let's not call it terrariumed. We'll still hold
the same escalator railings, ride in the same

commuter trains, carry the same signs and groceries
and guilt. We'll just snag a little less. Mothers,

I know we used to wander our dark like spelunkers.
I know we had head lamps and ropes. Like bats

we knew the pings of our limits, and unlike bats,
pushed past them. But now with the news alerts

buzzing. Now with that starving polar bear.
Now with the "Gun-Free Zone" signs on the doors

of the kindergarten. Now with everything balanced
on the thinnest of threads that we know not to test

for tension. So what if we armor ourselves
with horn sections? So what if we recite state capitals

in the shower's echo chamber, or avoid the sad
billboard eyes of the boat donation girl? So what

if sometimes we set down the armfuls of nails
and brambles, shut off the radio? We know

the shutting off is so we can listen. We know
the setting down is so we can pick up and carry.

Good Morning

Good morning, day full of soft, fine rain
gently ruining my red suede shoes.
Good morning, day in which I am not in a hospital,
or on the phone with a hospital,
or on the phone with an assisted living facility,
or on the phone with an insurance company or
funeral home or lawyer's office.
Good morning.
Good morning, day in which I feel guilty dropping off my oldest
child at school in new sneakers that are a little too big.
Good morning, companion guilt, guilt that walks next to me
and doesn't ask much.
Good morning.
Good morning, day hazed by a semi-sleepless night, day begun
when my youngest child woke at 5:30, and I held him in the dawn-
dark until he said "Out there? Out there?" like a cheerful parrot.
Good morning.
Good morning, obscure Elvis song on the radio reminding me
of that time I went to Graceland for laughs and ended up weeping.
I was 23 and foolish. Forgive me.
Good morning, day in which I can ask forgiveness again.
Good morning, papercut.
Good morning, small wound that will be gone by Saturday.
Good morning, chance again to read the book I've half-finished.
Good morning, chance again to feel that creeping dissatisfaction
at how I haven't yet finished the book.

But maybe tonight I will. Good morning, maybe tonight.
Good morning, sink full of dishes, spider web in the corner.
Good morning, house to which I'll in all likelihood
return later today, looking largely the same as when I left.
Good morning, likelihood.
Good morning.
Good morning.
Good morning.

HERE IN THE FUTURE WE ARE ALWAYS WATCHING OURSELVES

Once we walked next to a river full of yellow perch
and factory run-off and knew we were there.

We didn't consider backdrop or backlighting.
We walked. We fretted about the carcinogens.

We imagined being thirty, moving to Belgium.
Overhead a tree frog made its ridiculous small sound

and maybe we laughed, or maybe we welled up
for a second, the futility of that noise

against the river's steady pulse, but we heard it.
Once someone took a picture of us before

we were ready, standing by a lake, a dogwood,
a field of sunflowers, and it was two weeks until

we got that film developed, and then there we were
off-guard in front of some beautiful thing,

sharp-skinny or round with youth, hands
outspread in a strange almost-egret angle,

hair hanging to our waist, maybe, or buzzed
close like we did that summer, open-mouthed

as if we were saying something, which
we almost certainly were. Now we're never

saying something in the photos.
How powerful we are now. How careful.

The construction of a world requires
diligence. Is that tulip tree the best tulip tree?

Is that moon the best moon?
Do our crow's feet show, and if so,

is it in the most self-assured way? What about
the sky behind us, is it red enough for revelation,

are the streaks coming through?
Is that mountain significant enough?

We've seen others like it. These dandelions
are furred and lovely in the afternoon sun, but

our hands look old. Try again. When did
our skin start to gather like that?

When did the moon get so flawed? Look
at that photo by the lake, the tree, the field.

We were there once, and our hands,
our strange hands, were so perfect.

ENTREATY

Dear spring, commit. Burst
your bee-and-bloom, your blaze
of blue, get heady, get frocked,
get spun. Enough with your tentative
little breaths, your one-day-daffodils/
one-day-dewfrost. Honeysuckle us
right to our knees. Wake us
with your all-night mockingbirds,
your rowdy tree frogs. Gust
and dust us. Pollen-bomb the Hondas
and front halls, but please, no more
of this considering. This delicate-
tendrilling. Your pale green
worries me. Your barely-tuliped
branches, your slim shoots
any sideways look could doom.
The truth is I don't want to think
about fragility anymore. I can't
handle a blown-glass season,
every grass blade and dogwood
so wreckable. I'm trying hard
to teach the infallibility
of nightlights, to ignore the revving
of my own fallible heart. Spring,
you're not helping. Go all in.
Throw your white blossoms

into my gutters. Flood
my garage, mud my new shoes,
leave me afternoon-streaked
and sweating. Vine yourself
around me. Hold me
to you. Tighter.

Tunnel Vision

As in, the sky constricts. As in, a seagull's overhead
and then suddenly it's not, though it is.
All the senses short-sheeted. The distant car horn,

then six steps later the hollered rebuke. The soft brush
against your legs maybe fern, maybe fingers-
through-the-manhole-cover. Who could say.

Your mind is a dog with a rodent in its teeth,
a rodent named *Car Wreck*, a rodent named *Tumor*,
a rodent named *What Have You Done to Stop the Shootings?*

You celebrate the streaks: Twenty-Two Days
of Actually Seeing Contrails. Three-Plus Weeks
of Grapefruit Awareness. Then the inevitable

closing in, the whiting out, the low hum
that covers the plash of a kayak oar into the bay.
What oar? What kayak? What bay? You're afloat,

but buoyed on your own disasters, legless
because what use are legs in dread's waters?
On the shore someone has poured you a lemonade.

You've paddled back. You're drinking it.
You're smiling and saying words like *incumbent*
and *coleslaw* and *Harper Lee*, as the sweet drink

spills down through your bodiless body,
elegant machinery, remarkable scaffold that holds
nothing now but your pounding, pigheaded heart.

All 21 of Mississippi's Beaches Are Closed Because of Toxic Algae

—CNN headline

It begins with the sweetest
contaminant masks: houndstooth,

hummingbirds & hibiscus. The tagline:
Breathe us in on Instagram. It begins

with Instagram, the masks accented
by skateboards and gold-light

palmettos. It begins with a sister's
call from the car: *so many trees*

down from last night! In the backseat
the kids holler-sing. The weatherman

looks surprised by the tornado in Baltimore.
In Stanhope. In Bucks County, PA.

Strange days, folks. It begins with a gone
jetty. Gone campsite. Gone silo. It begins

with *did you see.* With *still? again?*
It begins with *I could swear it wasn't always.*

It begins and keeps beginning.
With a sidebar headline and a bummer

of a vacation week—no ocean this year,
sorry, kids. But let's not make it

worse with worry. We'll play more
mini-golf. We'll still have a good time.

WHAT WE INVENTED

Hybrid orchids. Hydrofoils. Zodiac signs.
We invented Friday, and June,
and All Hallows Eve. We invented flight

and then higher flight, so high we stopped
calling it *flight* and started calling it *orbit*.
We invented aquariums. We invented

all-night diners and the neon oasis
of their glow. We invented equations.
We invented skirts: mini, maxi, A-line, pencil.

Techniques to make skirts any color
we love. We did not invent love. We did not
invent regret. We did not, of course, invent

stingrays. We did not invent death or birth,
though we did invent sympathy cards
and birth announcements. We invented

entire hams wreathed in pineapple rings,
and we invented the idea of carrying them
on heavy platters to the grieving, and we

invented mini spinach quiches and weddings
at which to nosh them. We invented tuxedos.
We invented the word *nosh*, and every

other word. We did not invent the sheep
that allow us wool for pencil skirts, or the air
that leaves neon after the nitrogen

and oxygen and argon and carbon dioxide
are stripped away. We did not invent
pineapples. We did not invent grieving,

though we did invent hymns and chants
and lanterns to help navigate it. We did not
invent ourselves, not the collective-fact-of-us,

but we spend our days inventing—
a delicate rice soup for a sniffling daughter,
a pinecone bird feeder, a sentence written

in our own particular sloping hand that says
so sorry for your loss, the words themselves
nothing, but the O of each word a small bowl

into which we try to fold all our best inventions,
the silent and shimmering ones, the ones
for which we haven't invented names.

I SPEND MY DAYS PUTTING AWAY,

the small blue car here, the skipped
heartbeat there, everything
stowed and safe. I don't want

anyone tripping, or slipping
into that world that isn't this one.
Here the couch is rust-orange;

here my black coat is slung
over the piano bench that sags
with four decades of etudes

and Beginning Sonatinas.
Last month I had pneumonia.
My right lung rattled. I conducted

my household from the couch
with a baton of cough-paused words:
Both boys need baths. The robotics

field trip is tomorrow. Slowly
my cough subsided, but the damage
was done: the veil had thinned.

I could just make out the world
away from my house, its dark outlines
of no couch, no small blue car,

and so I organized the game closet.
So I wore a soft yellow sweater.
So I swiped on berry lip gloss,

soloed socks into the trash,
switched on lamp after lamp
after lamp. I made the house

hum with electricity and order.
Look, children, I've put all your Legos
into these bright plastic bins.

Look, I've put all the little pieces
of uncouch, uncar into old
shoeboxes labeled *Not Yet*

and tucked them under my bed.
In time, maybe, I'll forget
where I hid them.

Spaceship Earth

EPCOT

We've FastPassed it, that great golf ball just inside
the gates, so my son and I don't have to wait long
to tour all of human time. Inside, Phoenicians
invent the alphabet; Romans carry news

from chariots. The Library of Alexandria
burns, but only for 15 seconds and we're on
to the monastery, where animatronic monks
copy manuscripts. One monk has fallen

asleep on his desk. It's so peaceful inside
the dark globe, track softly thudding
beneath us, and I thrill as we pass marvel
after marvel. O beloved papyrus! O Gutenberg!

O telegraph! O mannequin children TV-rapt
as Neil Armstrong bounds and proclaims!
The music swells and I'm weepy in the dark.
Then we're in a garage where a man builds

a desktop computer. The narrator's voice
says *here we are*. Says this like she's announcing
a victory. Outside thousands of people crowd
the park's entrance, waiting to open their bags

and show there's no violence inside. Outside
it's 88 degrees in February. In the ride's
last moments, our car swivels backward
and we fall, slowly, slowly, down a tunnel of stars.

ooooo

QUIVER

I have forgotten how to be still
these years. The hallway needs

sweeping. I have so much
to say about the dogwoods.

Always my body is aquiver, or
more accurately, a quiver

full of bees, large and stingerless,
frantic with some urgent business

I can't understand. Always
there are limes to be purchased,

or dental insurance, or discount
aquarium passes. I have not

returned the library books yet,
but I will. It's on my list.

A friend posts a picture
of Puget Sound and how dare

I never have gone? How many
jaunts add up to all of them?

I walk, I walk, I walk, and
the neighborhood streets

are lined with crepe myrtles.
As I notice them, I notice

my noticing. My body buzzes.
Who should I call about

all this fuchsia? Someone,
surely, should be alerted.

LET SOMEONE SAY YOU ARE ELECTRIC

and you become electric, an eel
in the best possible way, flicking light
and sharp static wherever you toss
your tail. The whole room spins
to a stop to watch you laugh
with an amaretto sour in hand.
Your teeth so even, or so
charmingly not. Why not try
Gaelic, or string theory, why not
karaoke "Bohemian Rhapsody"?
Even your failures are arresting.
Let someone say you are electric
and the world, too, becomes electric,
every streetlamp humming not
with a harbinger of burnout
but with its own scarcely-contained
thrill, its desire for every person
moving through its yellow orb,
in particular you. Of course you.
You once-with-the-train-trestle.
You once-with-the-wolfhound.
You of the fascinating wrists
and boots, my god, the boots!
The hawks overhead—what balletic
wheeling. Your orange juice
a complex equation in your mouth.

Does it matter if the words never
lead to a large, soft bed?
Does it matter if the words
were said a decade ago
by someone whose middle name
you've forgotten? Does it matter
if you know the speaker, or ever did?
The words are what matter,
little diamonds in your hand. Here:
you are electric. Put that diamond
next to the others. Make a trail
of gleaming and follow it to yourself.

FROM *THE COMPENDIUM OF ROMANTIC WORDS:* HOWL

Verb; noun. Notable for its compact muscularity,
as a wolf's haunches double up to spring
and then the red carnage. The word looks like
the open mouth that sings it, and an open mouth
is, of course, an *infini entendre* of possibility. Mostly,
though, the power of the word rests in its suggestion
of desperation, such that one's body might howl
for another's, or, more frequently, such that
a forsaken one howls in the night like an animal
(*see: tired metaphor; see: still erotic*). Important:
the forsaken must tell the forsaker about the howling,
so that even if the forsaker is three states
or six rivers or nine mountains away, the howling
can still be heard, can vibrate all night inside
a suburban bedroom, so that the headlights slicing
through blinds become a full moon through pines,
so that even as the lights fade, the person lying
in bed, *supine*, one letter from *lupine*, can feel
haunted and hunted and whole.

Compound adjective. Notable for its two distinct halves,
like estranged siblings, the first now slothed
with lazy connotation (*see: beach read convention;
see: sad strip mall sex shop*), the second spectacled,
mousy with As and curfews. Together, though,
they glint like struck flint. Together, they're the spark
inside which the object of desire, until then
only a green coat, a nimble hand on a fretboard,
without warning says *Baudelaire* or *contrapuntal*
or *glottal stop* and suddenly the pines and semis
and waiting room magazines vanish, the finch-song
stops, the gossamer, tenuous thread that keeps world
bound to world snaps and floats noiselessly away.
Untethered thusly, the admirer may experience sudden
vertigo or nausea, may sustain invisible bruising,
invisible lacerations. The swiftness of onset can shock,
but shouldn't. W*hip*, after all, is another word
for *move quickly; smart*, another word for *hurt.*

FROM *THE COMPENDIUM OF ROMANTIC WORDS:* DELICATESSEN

Noun. Notable for a sibilant elegance heightened
by the suggestion of cured meats. Not *deli*,
a vulgar nickname, a fly-den, a swing-by, but
a long sigh of syllables, a time machine. Inside
its languid hiss: flannel suits, stenographer glamour.
When the word is uttered, a skyline materializes.
Shadows sift down. Caution: coworkers waiting
for coleslaw may glance sidelong and drift into desire.
Strangers may stammer and stare. Hunger governs
subtly (*see: subtext; see: pastrami-on-rye-in-lieu-of-teeth-
to-collarbone*). The bell that rings as the door opens
is a tiny secret symphony. A napkin to the corner
of a crooked mouth is a tie unloosed, a sensible shoe
finger-hooked then dropped. *Delicate*, of course,
means *fragile*. A word is a breakable world. The bell
will ring again on the exit. The lunch hour florescence
will blanche back to sunlight, fidelity, crosstown
traffic—but first, this final selection from the great
glass case: corned beef or egg salad, pimento loaf
or tongue (*see: delicacy; see: language; see: a tapering flame*).

From *The Compendium of Romantic Words:* Undone

Adj. Notable for its implications of sorcery.
As in, *she looked at me and I was undone.*
As in, *he said "recalcitrant" and I was undone.*
As in, a spell was cast and a net inside unraveled
and out spilled all the flashing silver fish of reason.
A freighted word, indicating an action thrumming
with intent: the clasp undone, the button undone,
the seatbelt undone through the fumbling.
Particularly potent when spoken directly
to the object of desire (*see: you have undone me.*)
Key risk: if the undoer is not mutually undone,
eventually the undoing will cease. When this occurs,
the undone will sometimes seek out James Bond
marathons and grocery delivery while outside
it snows or suns or hails with immaterial commitment.
This is the crisis moment for the undone, who must
immediately get a pet scorpion, book a cruise
to the Arctic Circle, take up aviation, anything at all
that will cause the heart to flood the heart again,
anything at all that stems from parsing the word
to its stripped-down core: *un* as in *not*, *done* as in *finished.*

Instructive Fable for the Daughter I Don't Have

Walk into the woods and keep walking.
The tall pines swing like curtains in the moonlight;
the moonlight swings like a drunk man on a ship.
Search for the place the jewels are hidden, a.k.a.
the dark-furred hollow. Search for the mirror
in the old oak. Search for The Stag Who Can Speak
to Girls Like You (his voice, the stories say, is like a river—
low, and full of deaths it can't help). Small animals
will serrate the silence with their chatter. Underfoot,
roots will crack like bones. Wear your hair uncovered.
Wear your mouth unset. You may not find
the jewels, the mirror, the stag. But you may find
a bare possum skull. You may find some eyeteeth
in a damp log. You may find a berry patch, but
with bullets in place of berries, silver sparks
in the nightgleam. Put all these things into your pockets
and keep walking. The grackles will tell you
This way out, this way out. Don't answer. Don't be turned.
You entered the woods lost. Leave that way.

In Early Motherhood I Lay Down Like a Cat Each Night,

half repose, half almost-
spring, ready to leap up, leap
after. I was electricity.
I was conducted by cries.
I learned to vanish
the paces between my bed
and the crib. I learned to vanish
doorknobs, darkness.
I never fumbled,
or stumbled into walls.
There were no walls,
or I had no body
to crash against them.
I was molecular,
ionized, I was only
nerves and milk and Now.
I slept on my back
with my glasses on.
I slept no fan, no hum.
I slept while rocking,
I rocked while asleep,
I never slept
but lay down each night
inside the purr
of my wired, ready heart.

GESTATIONAL SIZE EQUIVALENCY CHART

Your baby is the size of a sweet pea.
Your baby is the size of a cherry.
Your baby is the size of a single red leaf
in early September. Your baby is the size
of *What if.* The size of *Please Lord.*
The size of a young lynx stretching.
Heat lightning. A lava lamp.
Your baby is the size of every dream
you've ever had about being onstage
and not knowing your lines. Your baby
is the size of a can of Miller Lite.
Apple-picking. Google. All of Google.
Your baby is also the size of a googol,
and also the size of the iridescence
at a hummingbird's throat. Your baby
is the size of a bulletproof nap mat.
Cassiopeia on a cold night. The size
of the 1.5-degree rise in ocean temps
between 1901 and 2015. Your baby
is the size of the lie you told your mother
the night before Senior Skip Day, and
also the size of the first time you saw
a whale shark glide by, its gray heft
filling the tank's window, and also
the size of just the very best acorn.

Your baby is the size of the Mona Lisa.
The size of the Louvre. The size
of that moment in "Levon" when
the strings first kick in. Your baby
is the size of a baby-sized pumpkin.
A bright hibiscus. A door. Your baby
is the size of the Gravitron, and your fear
the first time you rode it that your heart
might drop right through your body,
and then your elation when it didn't,
when the red vinyl panels rose and fell
and you rose and fell with them.

Exhausted with a Three-Week-Old, I Make a Quilt of My Near-Hallucinations

A moth bumping softly against the closed window
I stitch to a memory of racetrack cheers
and loudspeaker crackles, which I stitch to that time
I ate tiramisu on the Grand Canal while a Neil Young
song plinked incongruously through tinny speakers
and I'm not sure that tiramisu was any better
than the tiramisu I had in Northumberland,
Pennsylvania but I was in Venice after all, and anyway,
I've lost the thread again. Which is all I do these days.
This morning I put the dishwasher detergent
in the refrigerator and then, telling my husband,
forgot the word *refrigerator*. The baby looks up,
crosses his gray-blue eyes, turtles his small head
forward. He is the most beautiful alien.
This house is silent for sleeping but no one sleeps.
So I stitch together the wind rustling the tall oaks
with the bells on the old wooden fire truck ride,
the one I rode, the one my sons will ride. I stitch
the ticking of April rain to midway dings
and buzzes, the piped-in nickelodeon.
I stitch the cat's mouth opening in a quiet click
to the clamor of Mardi Gras eve. I stitch
the dishwasher's low complaint right to that
Bourbon Street strip club pulse.
Here, in the hinterlands of sleeplessness,
every step feels like a moonwalk. Every time

I move one finger, another finger twitches.
So I stitch and stitch and cover myself
with my quilt and though it might look like I'm drifting
to sleep, I never am, because the baby
is awake again and his gray-blue eyes
are starting to focus on lamps and windows
and because every time I say *hush, hush*
I am really saying *world, come back, get loud.*

Love Poem with Planetary Wonders and Loose Definition

1.
Once we stood in our backyard in smalltown Missouri. We were
young and had grown our first garden, which I guess is a metaphor
though it was also an actual garden. The tomatoes were out of
control. The cucumbers, the cayennes, the pattypan squash like
elfin flying saucers. Hyacinths, hyacinths. Our grass wavered in
the midsummer swelter. Everywhere, mosquitos. Aphids dotted
the undersides of wide leaves but we didn't really mind. We
couldn't blame them for wanting to live in this hot green place.

2.
Once we walked barefoot through the surf at just-past-twilight,
the sky slipping toward navy. The moon, impassive and pink-tinted,
glinted off the water. *The strawberry moon*, named for June's ripening
fruits but clearly committing to its name. The cool air alchemized
the foam around our ankles to something warmer, softer. Beneath
our feet, sand shifted; in the ocean beside us, unseen dolphins dove,
caught fish, slept with their gentle eyes open.

3.
Once we hiked the Broken Arrow trail in Sedona's late spring
quiet. The light ambered around us as we passed cactus flowers
and juniper, a vast sinkhole named the Devil's Dining Room. On
a warm wide rock we rested and looked out: the red land to all

sides, the blue overhead so absolute it seemed impossible the day would end. The sun settled on us like a great cat, dozing.

1a.

A shadow crossed the garden and we looked up from our tomato-picking to see the bright bulbs of the hot air balloons—red, yellow, green—cresting the late afternoon. They were right there, so close we could see the riders in the baskets. The whole day tilted. We waved, and with our free hands reached for each other, stood there under the sky now strange with color and occasional flame.

2a.

I'm sure we could hear the stern *hush hush* of the waves against the shore, but what I remember are the sounds from the boardwalk behind us: the scream-pause-scream of the Sea Dragon riders, the tinny horse race game call-to-post, the bell after bell signaling Whack-a-Mole winner, squirt gun race winner, winners, winners, all. We stood and summer floated to us, gold and brash and ringing.

3a.

And when we made it back to the trailhead we were desert-dusted and sweaty, so we drove downtown to a coffee shop and sat out back under umbrellas drinking our iced lattes, looking at the wild rocks, the wild creosote, and later that night we went to a gallery and saw a mosaic that cost more than the house we'd just bought, and later that night we lay in our motel bed listening to the anonymous children on the floor above us tramping like small elephants, and later that night we slept the sleep of glad people, and we were glad.

4.

Darling, here is a sky polluted with our city. Kiss me under it.

ENOUGH

I got here through no talent of my own.
I did not birth myself, or even will myself
into being. One day I was a cluster of cells,
one day I was a heart, one day I was
a human in the world. Now what? Look
at the luck I was given, born into a place
with a hot yellow sun. Born with two
nimble hands, a strong enough voice.
If I'm not shouting down cruelty or at least
singing all the time, what am I doing?
If I'm not building a table or holding a child
or slicing tomatoes warm from the garden
I've weeded myself, what am I doing?
I bought these electric blue flats. Suede.
I did it because it made me feel a little
happy, that small dopamine hit that comes
from picturing yourself looking like someone
someone wants to look at. But how absurd
is that? How flimsy? I've never learned to change
a tire. My music theory is abysmal.
Sometimes I don't realize it's snowing until
there's already a dusting on the driveway,
which is certainly close to excuseless.
But I swear I'm mainly paying attention.
I swear I'm grateful at least a dozen times a day.
If I could cradle the earth in my hands

for ten seconds, I would, just to show it how
tenderly I could hold it, how I wouldn't drop it,
how I cherish it even as I'm turning in early
instead of going out to see the Perseids.
I've always loved a carnival. Is it enough
to love a carnival? I could ride the teacups
all day. That shriek that comes from spinning,
the one that unfurls from somewhere deep
below the throat like a bright streamer?
It's language. It translates into *thank you.*

ABECEDARIAN FOR THE DANGEROUS ANIMALS

All frantic and drunk with new warmth, the bees
buzz and blur the holly bush.
Come see.
Don't be afraid. Or do, but
everything worth admiring can sting or somber.
Fix your gaze upward and
give bats their due,
holy with quickness and echolocation:
in summer's bleakest hum, the air
judders and mosquitoes blink out,
knifed into small quick mouths. Yes,
lurking in some unlucky bloodstreams
might be rabies or histoplasmosis, but almost
no one dies and you
owe the bats for your backyard serenity.
Praise the cassowary, its ultraviolet head, its
quills and purposeful claws. Only one
recorded human death, and if a boy
swung at you, wouldn't you rage back? Or *P.*
terribilis, golden dart frog maligned by Latin,
underlauded and unsung, enough poison to
vex two elephants into death but ardent
with eggs and froglets, their protection a neon
xyston. And of course,
yes, humans. Remarkable how our
zeal for safety manifests: poison, rifle, vanishment.

Tether Me

Dear high school marching band drum line
cadencing through the summer evening
from a mile away, please hold me here.
Let your sound so gold and bright
be a tether. Keep me from drifting again
into that space where I don't know anything
but the earthquake magnitude of my love
for my loves and the spidersilk thin web
by which I'm knotted into my life. Dear UPS
delivery knock, remind me of where I live—
this sturdy house with a red door,
an aging roof. Dear telemarketer, thank you
for pulling me back from the antigravity.
Who can sustain in that vast floating, so full
of stars but endless? Dear public radio
segue music, hook and hold me. Dear hashtag,
dear late night sketch, dear photo of a friend's
new pitbull pup, truss me right to this earth.
Dear caterwauling fire truck in my rearview.
Dear tailless calico peering in my window.
Dear child needing milk or Goldfish
or to know how eardrums work, let me sit
on the kitchen floor with you. Let's notice how
we're both right here. Dear automatic car lock,
as I'm walking away, I'll press the button.
Honk once to remind me I haven't disappeared.

THE MYSTERIES

I used to be closer to the mysteries.
Someone said there was peace in an acorn
and I believed it. A book told me if I
ate the cold I could love it, and so I tried it,
and so I could. I still carried fear,
but there were these long moments
of slanted light and far-away train sounds,
or constellations above a wide, slow river,
and those long moments held the part of me
that could say yes to things like ghosts
and prayer and the belief that desire
could move people like chess pieces.
Sometimes I cupped my hands
around the moon, not to catch it but
to hold it still long enough to thank it.
I believed I could hold it still.
I believed it wanted my thanks.
I knew crickets then, though to be fair
they usually hummed a Lou Reed song
or said *dear girl, dear girl* or something
else that now I'm tempted to dismiss
as nonsense. But what do I know now?
Once I carried a vast, calm lake inside me,
and sometimes, yes, it was on fire, but
I sat with the flames. And it wasn't always

on fire. Sometimes it was just vast, and dark,
and clear, and it held everything—
darting fish, constellations, ghosts. I believed
in ghosts then. It seemed possible
to be so much a part of this place
that it would never let you go.

CHADWICK LAKE, 8:15 A.M.

You're trying to make the lake
something it isn't. You're trying
to make it a mirror, a meditation,
a mother. You're trying, at least,
to make it a lake, but it isn't even that.
It's a half-lake, at best. It's half-filled
with cattails and sludge. There's a white bag
caught in the weeds. A bright yellow
bulldozer where there should be glint
and mallards. Why can't you be
satisfied with the not-quite lake?
What are you still hoping might
surprise you? Why do you persist
in looking for a crisp mountain sky
when you know you live half
a country from the mountains?
Why are you always waiting for that day
in late October when the leaves
and the air and the distant hay smell
are all in exact and perfect proportion
to one another? Don't you know
that's a sure way to go through life
as if you've swallowed a tiny burning marble?
Look at these tread marks in the mud,
aren't they their own small arrows of beauty?

Look at those cattails, don't they bend like
any meadow flower or Adirondack fern?
So what if the ducks have flown off?
So what if the turtles have vanished?
Can't you love the black plastic construction
fence, the diggers, the plumes of exhaust?
The white bag keeps blowing, though
there's no wind today. You walk closer.
It's an egret. Its long neck curved to preen,
feathers bright as the camera's flash
at the moment everyone says *surprise*.

Poem for Quicksand

O you gorgeous torture, you slow-mo sadist,
you taught me all I knew about breathlessness.

You sucked the air from the room each time
cartoons zoomed to you. You sucked the air

from me. The secret of you, the lying-in-wait
of you, the no-one-safe of you. Quicksand,

I wanted things, too. I was a child made
of silt and agitation. Built of granules

of guilt. I knew the ways to escape you—
the arms-out dead-mans-float, a stoic cool,

a steady climb—but I knew, too, that these
were fools' techniques, like a school desk

for an atom bomb, designed to calm
a right-on panic. It was your tenacity

that drew me, the way you bided, silent,
then swallowed whole, your hunger absolute.

I knew you'd never let go. I knew because
already my bones were dense with you.

I KEPT GETTING BOOKS ABOUT BIRDS

as if recognizing the yellow-winged one
at the feeder, the shiny black one hopping
through the grass might somehow
become enough. As if knowing *magpie* or *thrush*
or *prothonotary warbler* might give me a handle
of sorts, something to hold as all around me
the books piled up and the hours, too,
time unrolling like a lush carpet
that caught me again and again,
a foot sinking into the plush and there went
three hours, six days, half a year.
I kept getting books about birds as if
in the Great Ledger of What I Had Accomplished
I could simply fill in some Latin names
and notes on skeletal pneumaticity
and be done. I kept getting books about birds
because those days I had no reason
to go to bed and so the night stretched
and yawned and stayed awake,
because my corn-fritters-from-scratch
didn't pan out, because the garden had all
the hot peppers the neighborhood could eat
but the tomatoes stayed hard and green
no matter how I coaxed them, because
I wanted to write a novel but never made it
past a protagonist, because I wanted

to understand how some people galloped
through their lives as if they were astride
tall white horses and here I was
spending my drawn-out days researching
ailments and likelihoods. I kept getting
books about birds, and they were beautiful,
the books, glossy and thin, and I looked
at them, and I stroked their smooth covers,
but I'd be lying if I said I ever read one.
They were so dull, with their migration
pattern charts and seed particulars,
and I knew as I looked at the congregating
backyard starlings or whatever they were
that the only real solution was to walk outside
and startle them so that they rose in one
of their gorgeous rivers, one of their gorgeous
bed sheets, one of their gorgeous
choreographies of shadow, and to see, at last,
in that one bright, cacophonous moment
something I had made.

Dear Place, I Ask So Much

Canyon me. Ravine me. Redwood me,
roots deep to the wet center. Limb me

cloudward. Fan me out alluvial
and unabashed. My soft heart sediment.

My hard heart anthracite. Lagoon me.
Lava me. Lake me sprawling and still.

Dear beasts in the tar pits, these millennia!
Dear glass-cased specimens, how little we knew!

I dream a tattoo, a cerulean speck
on my forearm: our planet from four billion

miles away. Trench me deep, O
earth-and-more. Volcano me to sky

or under sea. High desert me.
Dell and dune me. Hurricane me

homeward. Whitecap me out
of my small fretting, magnolia me

away from what mires. Oh home-of-lynx,
home-of-grackle, home-of-frog-and-fox.

What incantation can I weave for you?
What spell can I spin to glacier you

again blue and unending?

ooooo

FABLE FOR THE FINAL DAYS

In the end it was an asteroid,
a great mass of iron and nickel
and cobalt and terminal velocity

that plummeted our planet
into the violet forever, stripped
our sky of both sun and moon,

brought on the coughing, the fires,
the birds carpeting interstates,
the brief run on gas masks, then

guns, then cudgels, the one
satellite radio station playing
"Nothing Compares 2 U" on repeat

for four days until the static,
the board games while we waited—
Clue, Battleship, Sorry—and the heat

rising and rising and our houses
shuddering, and the burials, and then
the streets humped with bodies,

no weeping after a couple of weeks,
and then no people at all, just
the burrowing animals tentatively

nosing into homes, the foxes
and chipmunks, the hungry badgers,
and then their stillness, too,

curled under cars, only the soil
still sizzling with roaches and earwigs
as the whole earth softened

into fur and dirt and crumbling,
as lichens grew gently over
law firms, as mothers turned

to bones and then to loam,
and if you were to come back
here today, the ground beneath

your feet would stir and shift,
and though you would not
know the story of this place,

you might feel that yielding
and tread carefully, you might
tread, even, with tenderness.

PLEASE LET IT BE ALIENS

"A solar observatory in New Mexico is evacuated for a week and
the FBI is investigating. No one will say why." *—Washington Post*

Let it be a silver disc, a foil zeppelin
bleeping across the radar, a blot
in front of the sun
and then gone.
Let the word *intergalactic*
be paired at last with *espionage*.
Let uniformed men stride briskly
down long corridors, let astronomers
pace and calculate.
Let there be phone calls and code words,
an envelope unsealed
by trembling hands,
and let the light become strange,
the radio signals scramble,
the dogs whine skyward.
Let there be a great silver crack
down the sky of our surety,
and flames, and fear
borne of wonder. O, let it
be aliens for once, instead of another
threat from our own sad-sack planet,
a call-from-inside-the-house twist
we all see coming.

Let us believe,
though it seems impossible,
that someone still wants to claim us,
someone still thinks our poison-
green world worth wanting.

On the Issue of Lunar Trash

Dear moon, forgive us the tie tack, the falcon feather.
Forgive us the golden olive branch. Our wish for peace

is our wish, not yours. You had peace, and now you have
an olive branch. Moon, what will you do with our hundred

two-dollar bills? Moon, forgive us the watchband. The hammer.
The Bible, as if you're the one seeking your own source.

All the cameras. All the antennae. The nail clippers.
Oh moon, you're literally holding our shit—we couldn't

be bothered to cart it back to our own atmosphere.
Moon, once we stabbed a flag into you, as if you loved

our country, any country. You were absence of color and then
we pocked you all silver and red and blue. You were stillness

and then we kicked up dust that had never known anything's kick.
Moon, once all our wreckage was a world away, and then

we appeared with our tripods and canisters, our larks
and catchphrases. I think, moon, that you must hate us.

Your molten mantle must roil, your iron core seethe.

You crest the dark sky over my house and your face

looks the worst kind of disappointed, like a mother when
her children have bloodied each other's tender bodies.

Moon, say it's all right. Say you understand. Look at me—
freighting you with a mouth I've invented just so I can hear it

say *forgive*. Oh moon, say you'll forgive me for that, too.

SHELL GAME

We slide and patter, we lift and reveal.
Inside the nutshell is a pea.
Inside the pea is a shell. Inside the shell
is a matryoshka doll, and inside that
is another, and inside that is your country
that maybe you once thought was all
endless blue and mountains, but surprise—
it was always inside something.
Watch the slide, watch the slide!
We hide the melting seasons under
treason and voila, you're out 20 bucks
and the icecaps. Or we switch it—
doesn't matter. In this game, everything
is the right size both to hide
and be hidden. It doesn't matter how
closely you follow: the fix is in
and you're out of luck, the pea
palmed and gone. We fold the table
quick, and snatch the bills, skilled
as surgeons. We can't be caught.
We're the tosser, the shill, the lookout,
and the cop. We're the shell and the pea.
The wooden doll. The country.

ALTERNATIVE FACTS

Here is a frog. So it has wings.
It's a winged frog. So it's red—
some frogs are. So it's sitting
in a branch of this elm—so what?
It likes elms. Or it's a cardinal-frog,
or a cardinal, but what's the difference,
really? Anyway, check out this elm.
Go on and climb it. Great view.
So it has no leaves, so what? So it has
no branches. So it's fiberglass
and steel, so what? You're up there
now, aren't you? Off in the distance,
see the ocean? Blue as the sky
and full of dolphins. So? An ocean
can be a parking lot. It's a metaphor,
jesus. And *dolphins* means *shopping carts*,
try to keep up. Come down now,
you've seen enough. You look nauseous,
you must be hungry—here, have
an apple. Fine, it's a skull, but listen
to that crunch, and you wouldn't believe
the phosphorus. Lower your voice,
someone might hear. Just joking,
your voice is a blown dandelion,
and that's not a metaphor—
look at your protests fuzzing

the metal leaves of the elm. Relax.
Why so hung up on definitions?
Look around. Your dog is a coal mine.
Your bedroom is seven globes
and a Hail Mary. Try to enjoy yourself.
Let's try a game. Close your eyes,
which are conch shells, and count
to five, which goes *silver-Virginia-acrylic-
lemon-moon*. Now keep them closed.
Good—you're finally getting it.

POEM WRITTEN AFTER THE SUPREME COURT CONFIRMATION VOTE

The man's yelling—guttural, angry—stopped me
on the acorn-littered street until I realized it was just Bob Seger

singing "Old Time Rock & Roll" in someone's open garage.
I was walking at dusk and maybe I was a little jumpy.

The votes came in a few days ago, and what we thought
would happen did. In my house I'm the only girl,

my sons remind me. Even the hermit crab is a boy,
we think. It's such a good house: these people I love,

the little orange Halloween lights twinkling over the piano,
the yellow mums. But my house is only one house,

and I have been in other houses. My neighborhood
has 228. Last month my youngest and I took

an evening stroll. At the far end of our street, three cop cars,
an ambulance, red lights strobing the softening sky.

A teenager driving past slowed. *There's a lady sitting
on the curb*, he said. *She looks like she's been beat up.*

Oh, I said, *thanks.* My son, who had been watching
squirrels, asked me why the ambulance was there.

An accident, I said, and he understood that,
and we walked home, the cicadas screaming

from the pines as if someone had wronged them.

Danger Days

when the combination of heat and humidity makes it feel
like 105°F or hotter

In the movies from the eighties, children
wore red pants and wild hair.
They were always circling cul-de-sacs
on banana-seat bikes, always wandering
after dark into woods full of hoots
and clicks. What haunted me more
than the ghoul-girls or gloved slashers

were the missing parents—not dead, usually,
just elsewhere. When the séance began
innocently, when the doll's eyes popped open,
the grown-ups were never around.
They were off smoking pot,
they were date-nighting, affair-having.
They were office-stuck, their kids set
with house keys and frozen Salisbury steaks.
Sometimes they were home but sleeping,
snug and unghosted. Wherever they were,

they weren't watching. We don't live
on a cul-de-sac, so my kids ride their bikes
in a long, slow loop up our driveway
and back. I'd like to send them

rocketing down our tree-named streets—
Oakwood, Elmridge—but the main road
is Shadow Pines, and I've seen enough
movies to know what that means. I think

of those gone grown-ups a lot now.
When the latest mass shooting alert pings.
When ire is gilded again into policy.
Tonight the weatherman says
Three danger days in the next week,
the heat a mouth closed around our state.
Outside, the humidity moans.
Trees grow talons. My husband and I
are up late again, watching the news
while our children sleep. We're here
in our house off Shadow Pines, here
in the first part of a century bent
toward flaming out. Dear children
of the eighties, across the dark
country, phones and laptops and TVs
flicker. We're watching now,
room after room after room.
Dear children of the eighties, can you
tell us now what was in the woods?
Can you tell us if watching
stopped anything from happening?

LET ME TRY TO EXPLAIN MY NIGHTS

If you can imagine the clatter
when the bone china shelf collapses,
or the world-rekiltering when the parakeet

you thought was mute yellow sweetness
starts screaming obscenities in a sailor voice,
then you can imagine how I feel

some nights. Like my life is still right here,
still the one through which I move
quite capably from dawn until

the silent time, but then in the silent time
all I can think about are the ones making the silence,
and if I could keep everyone safe forever

just by touching them, I would grow
a thousand hands, but I know how
lucky I am to have the hands

I do, and how do I explain this? Look—
outside the stars are cold and ringing
in their great black bell and I can't

do a thing for them. My voice could never
reach them, not even if a voice could
speed across years of light. But some

things I can control if I do everything
exactly right. So it's night and I'm checking
the stove again, *off off off off*, I'm checking

the garage, I'm unplugging the toaster
that's been on the fritz, I'm blocking
the front door with the piano bench,

I'm thinking *tomorrow I'll eat more
blueberries, more spinach*, I'm circling back
to the stove. I always touch the burners.

I know a mistake would blister.
In the dark, though, it seems reasonable
to touch them, just to make sure.

POEM FOR THE WOODS

Not as I would dream them now, not with growls
and twig snaps, not with dark birds and thorned vines

I've invented (*keening blackwing, violencia*). Not late-day-
blood-sun-dappled, not refuge of men equipped

with knives and lust, not a mouth into which you might
venture and not return, no, nothing like that.

This is a poem for the woods as I knew them,
shaded and cool behind the Novaks' house.

They seemed endless, but there was a shortcut
to Fairblue Swim Club. They held no growls,

no spikes. Only squirrels skittering, plunking acorns
down the canopy. We'd been warned of poison ivy,

but never found it. We'd been warned of rotten limbs,
but none fell. One muddy, sun-laced afternoon, we took salt

from the pantry and ventured out to where the rocks
teemed with slugs. I'd like to say our cruelty

had to do with power—human girls versus torpidity—
but really it was our curiosity, pure and unnuanced.

We wanted to see mineral against membrane.
We wanted to see something living melt. If I could,

I'd find my younger self in those woods and stop her.
I'd say, *Someday you'll carry your cruelties with you*

and you'll never be able to set them down. Keep walking now.
Keep pretending you know of nothing but kindness.

ALL OF THIS BUILDING

You have me, I said, snug in my kindness,
and he replied *That's not enough,* and then
the house, the mini-blinds, the swivel chair
in which I was sitting blinked off and there I was
floating in black space. A few seconds later,
the dog barked and the house reappeared
and that was that. But I'd seen the vanishing.
It wasn't a cruelty, those words.
I wasn't and am not enough. No one is
and nothing. The maples aren't enough.
The Hammond organ solo isn't enough.
The neighborhood glassed and gleaming
after an ice storm, my husband's hand
on my hip in sleep, the Perseids, the napes
of my sons' necks, ice water in a metal cup,
my sister's scraping laugh—none of it is enough.
None of it on its own can keep the world
from blinking off, and it's always blinking off,
every day these million wreckages, these million
acts of attrition. But when my husband rests
his hand on my hip, something is built.
When I close my eyes inside the wavering song,
something is built. When my son opens
his door in the morning and comes to look for us,
when the street smells like charcoal and laundry,
when the weather sirens whine to silent,

when the dog barks his sharp gold bark,
something is built. The world is always leaving us
and so we build it back. We are tireless.
We are working even in our dreams.
All of this so that we have swivel chairs
and maples, so that we have a way to sleep,
a way to keep waking, a way to open doors
in the morning and walk out into a long dark
hallway, somehow more expectant than afraid.

POEM FOR RIGHT NOW

In protest I say the word *iridescent*.
In protest I say the word *vesper*.
In protest I say that I am in love
with this day, this exact day, this rain
on the thousands of dead leaves
in my backyard and the mourning dove
and the faint growl of the garbage truck
a few blocks over. I am in love with it.
In fucking love. It's true that
a mushroom cloud billows behind my eyes
most days. It's true I fall asleep drafting letters
in my language of pitchforks.
I know the chopping block is vast. I know
it has room and stomach for everything.
But my tongue and my head are mine.
So in protest I say the word *liquefy*.
In protest I say the word *gloaming*.
In protest I will remember how once
my friend and I walked through an alley
in a strange city, and my friend wore
a paper dragon in her hair, and the city
was five o'clock gold all around us.
In protest I say the word *dragon*.
There are days I've carried like candles
to light the rest of my life, and I will not
set them down. Watch me hold

a decade-ago snow night, moon-bright
and silent, right next to my hammering rage.
Watch me house *halcyon* next to *senator*,
lagoon next to *constituent*. I am trying
to become a contradiction machine.
I am poorly oiled, but every day I creak
awake again. The rain is heavy now
against my screened-in porch,
and the gutter that years ago my husband
patched with duct tape is still holding.
At this point, *repaired* is more accurate
than *patched*. It's still holding, and in protest
I marvel over that. In protest I marvel.
In protest I say *incandescent, liminal, charcuterie,*
embrace. I think *acquiescence* is a beautiful word,
too, but in protest I put it away. There are
other beautiful words. Like *lunar*. Like
resistance. Like *love*, like fucking *love*.

VESPERS

Mississippi at the end of March
is a chaos of wisteria. Someone
is grilling; someone is practicing
the clarinet. Next door the pugs
talk in their small, polite barks.
It's beer weather again. Time
again to eat berries so bright
we almost remark on it, but don't.
From the backyard hammock,
the early evening sky, blue
like a chlorine pool, is wreathed
by pines, catalpas, birds
insistent and fierce. It's easy
to forget we're only pretending
their language into song.
Even the power lines look kindly,
generously dividing the lushness
into manageable segments.
The fact that we can love it
so absolutely knowing that
we will absolutely leave it
is more remarkable than any
lightning storm or planet.
And also less: everyone swims
through this same brightdark water,
and no one asks for praise.

But I see you—you, somehow
nowhere close to collapsing
inside the incomprehensible. I see you.
And you deserve the red berries,
the dark chocolate stout.
You deserve whatever fractured music
the air carries toward you.

ALL THE DEAD ANIMALS

The highway's asphalt smudged
with tragic beagles and armadillos,

deer who staggered to the median—
we know those. The avian accidents,

too: cardinal who mistook glass for sky,
small naked robin on the sidewalk.

But what about the ones who kept
surviving? Where is the gray squirrel

gone grayer until its acorn-heart
stopped? The long-lived mallard

who floated one day into no-day?
Where are their soft, still bodies?

It makes sense, or I want it to:
the animals take such care not to die.

Every summer I walk by Silver Lake,
its bank shining with sunning turtles

—snappers, red-eared sliders—
and when I pass they slip noiselessly

into the water. I want to believe that
some wild things go to death only

if they're chased there. I want
to believe in some vast secret

forest where lucky old hawks
hunt forever and elderly coyotes doze

in a clearing. I could never visit,
I know. But somehow that place

would gentle my own life. Its teeth
and instinct. Its hackles. Its flight.

Everything Mattered/Matters/Will Matter

Like last night, when the astronaut described
sunrise in space and showed Soyuz rocket selfies,
and I didn't make my son go with me to the talk
because it was pouring, and that was either
a good decision or a bad one.

Like the Clementines on the kitchen island.

Like the kitchen island piled with junk mail
and Valentines and chargers and Clementines
and how I always want it clean and how
I also know enough to think *this is the time
in my life when the kitchen island is never clean.*

Like the blue swing bending
the sodden backyard branch,
and how it's been there years too long
but my sons will likely remember
its plastic bucket seat, its accumulated
leaves and dirt, and how they spun.

Like moss.

Like ibises.

Like the massive Caspian tiger, extinct.

Like the live tiger my sons and I watched
pace at the base of fake temple ruins
in an Orlando theme park.

Like the carbon footprint of flying
from Birmingham to Orlando
and how I bought the tickets anyway,
how each day I hurt the earth more
but there are live tigers still
roaming fake temple ruins
and I want my children to see them.

Like how I know this is the attitude
that gave us albatross skeletons
bright with soda caps and Bic lighters.

Like albatross skeletons.

Also like albatrosses.

Like Saturday's forecast map,
with its Severe Weather Outlook,
our town the orange iris
in the snake eye of risk.

Like *Where is your other shoe?*

and *Can you pick up milk?*
and *I thought we were enrolled in autopay*
and *Is your backpack still in the car?*
and *Can you grab me a pen?*
and *Can I have another pancake?*
and *Baby, can you find the Lego guy's head?*
and *Here you go*
and *Here you go*
and *Here you go*

Like this rain that won't stop.

Also how the forecast says
that it will stop on Sunday.

WE LIVE IN THE MOST EXQUISITE TERRARIUM

The fresh macadam is glossed with rain
and from the roadside, garden zinnias shout
their unabashed reds and fuchsias.

In a department store, a man
deftly arranges lipsticks by gradations
of purple, Velvet Violet to Punch-

Drunk Plum. A college radio deejay
follows new folk with old punk;
she knows it's important to keep

the airwaves sparking. This yard is soft
with Bermuda grass. This yard is coarse
with tall fescue. Look at our Climate

Controlled Storage Units. Look at
our socks rolled together in pairs.
Look at the emails we've crafted

in order to make someone think of us
once the lights go out. We curate
this place with such care. As if there's

nothing outside its blue dome. Or
as if we get to stay in here forever.

WORK

I think at first it's a mob outside my window—
those guttural, punctuated punches of voice.
I think this even as I sit alone in my office
on a deserted spring break campus in the middle
of spring. It's the middle of spring and I'm primed
to hear epithets in sparrow calls. It's work these days
to hear a bird for a bird, a voice for a voice.
In my own house a door slams, and my heart
is off like a stallion because lately so many guns
have been firing where you least expect them.
We don't own any, but so what, these days?
Last week a transformer blew one block over—
a loud, low boom, birds scattering through
the neighborhood—and ten minutes later
there were two cops on my street. A neighbor
had heard violence, too. Sometimes I'm so deep
down the tunnel that my name, bright and certain
as a sunflower, startles me into a cry,
and then it's *sorry* and a careful laugh
to my wide-eyed children, and then the work
of climbing out, hand over hand through the dark
humming. I remind myself our names exist
and they are bright names. I remind myself
for every person razing there's another engineering
a ladder of light. I remind myself about Mount Rose
and Lake George and the Atlantic where

I learned to dive through gray-green waves,
and then I'm back to the seagulls I sometimes
mistake for sirens, their long shrieks barbed
in my head. But the sun on the boardwalk
is white as wings, and I work my way back
and back to it. Out my window, the chanting
is getting closer, spiked and steady. I squint
until I see it: a yellow digger, caterpillar-treading
up the empty street. It grunts and barks. It sounds
like violence but look at it. Look. It's coming
to make something. It's coming to work.

PLANET

This morning this planet is covered by winds and blue.
This morning this planet is lit with dustless perfect light,
enough that I can see one million sharp leaves
from where I stand. I walk on this planet, its hard-packed

dirt and prickling grass, and I don't fall off. I come down
light if I choose, heavy if I choose. I never float away.
Sometimes I want to be weightless on this planet, and so

I wade into a brown river or dive through a wave
and for a while feel nothing under my feet. Sometimes
I want to hear what it was like before the air and so I duck
under the water and listen to the muted hums. I'm ashamed

to say that most days I forget this planet. That most days
I think about dentist appointments and plagiarists
and the various ways I can try to protect my body from itself.

That last weekend I saw Jupiter through a giant telescope,
its storm stripes, four of its 67 moons, and was filled
with fierce longing, bitter that instead of Ganymede or Europa,
I had only one moon floating in my sky, the moon

called Moon, its face familiar and stale. But this morning
I stepped outside and the wind nearly knocked me down.
This morning I stepped outside and the blue nearly

crushed me. This morning this planet is so loud with itself—
its winds, its insects, its grackles and mourning doves—
that I can hardly hear my own lamentations. This planet.
All its grooved bark, all its sand of quartz and bones

and volcanic glass, all its creeping thistle lacing the yards
with spiny purple. I'm trying to come down light today.
I'm trying to see this place even as I'm walking through it.

Acknowledgments

I am grateful to the editors of the following publications where these poems first appeared, sometimes in different form.

32 Poems: "Entreaty"

The Academy of American Poets Poem-a-Day: "High Dangerous"

The Adroit Journal: "All the Dead Animals"

American Poetry Review: "Anthropocene Pastoral," "Prayer," "Shell Game"

The Believer online: "In Early Motherhood I Lay Down Like a Cat Each Night"

Bennington Review: "Abecedarian for the Dangerous Animals," "Fable for the Final Days"

Blackbird: "From *The Compendium of Romantic Words*: Delicatessen," "From *The Compendium of Romantic Words*: Undone"

The Cincinnati Review: "All of This Building"

Colorado Review: "Instructive Fable for the Daughter I Don't Have"

Copper Nickel: "In Praise of the Horror Movie," "Poem for the Woods"

Crazyhorse: "Pillow Talk"

diode: "Exhausted With a Three-Week-Old, I Make a Quilt of My Near Hallucinations," "Let Me Try to Explain My Nights," "Let someone say you are electric," "Love Poem with Planetary Wonders and Loose Definition"

FIELD: "Enough," "Tunnel Vision," "We Live in the Most Exquisite Terrarium"

Five Points: "Strategies for Mothers in the Age of This Age"

Gettysburg Review: "I Kept Getting Books About Birds"

Gulf Coast: "The Guilt Depot"

Kenyon Review Online: "From *The Compendium of Romantic Words*: Howl," "From *The Compendium of Romantic Words*: Whip-Smart"

Los Angeles Review: "In Which the Country Is an Abandoned Amusement Park," "Spaceship Earth"

Love's Executive Order: "Alternative Facts"

Memorious: "Here in the Future We Are Always Watching Ourselves"

The Missouri Review: "Danger Days," "Inheritance," "Vespers," "What We Invented"

The Nation: "All 21 of Mississippi's Beaches Are Closed Because of Toxic Algae," "How Becoming a Mother Is Like Space Travel"

Orion: "Work"

Pleiades: "Poem Written After the Supreme Court Confirmation Vote"

A Public Space: "Poem for Quicksand"

The Rumpus: "Poem for Right Now," "Tether Me"

The Shore: "Dear Place, I Ask So Much," "Gestational Size Equivalency Chart"

Southern Indiana Review: "Good Morning," "The Mysteries"

The Southern Review: "Planet," "Please Let It Be Aliens"

Thrush: "Chadwick Lake, 8:15 a.m."

Waxwing: "On the Issue of Lunar Trash"

"I Kept Getting Books About Birds" appears in *Pushcart Prize XLIII*.

"Poem for the Woods" appears in *Pushcart Prize XLV*.

Thank you, always, always, to my parents and sister, whose support of my work from the very beginning has meant everything, and to everyone I am so very lucky to call family.

Thank you to the National Endowment for the Arts, the Sustainable Arts Foundation, and the Virginia Center for the Creative Arts for the grants and time to write that helped make many of these poems possible.

I am grateful to Traci Brimhall, Erika Meitner, and Marcus Wicker for their generosity, their time, and their poems.

Thank you to David Curran for allowing me to use for the cover of this book his remarkable heatmap visualization of the world's temperature anomalies each month since 1850 (data: HadCRUT4). A link to the full graphic can be found at catherinepierce.net.

Thank you to my wonderful and talented colleagues and students at Mississippi State University.

Boundless gratitude to Henry Israeli, Christopher Salerno, Rebecca Lauren, and everyone at Saturnalia Books.

Thank you to the friends who have read drafts/talked with me about making art/generally provided the camaraderie and support and small/large joys that have helped me get these poems written, in particular Maggie Smith, Nicky Beer, Brian Barker, Amy Wilkinson, Nathan Oates, Emily Spivack, Ian Chillag, Chris Coake, Stephanie Lauer, Richard Lyons, Becky Hagenston, Troy DeRego, and Mike Kardos.

Thank you, most of all and always, to Sam and Wyatt and Mike, all of whom have transformed my life in the best and deepest ways and made me happier than I ever knew was possible. S & W, you are remarkable humans and I am so, so lucky to be your mom. Mike, *thank you* doesn't even come close. Neither does *love*. But words are what I've got, and so they're yours.

Also by Catherine Pierce:

The Tornado Is the World

The Girls of Peculiar

Famous Last Words

Danger Days is printed in Adobe Caslon Pro.

www.saturnaliabooks.org